A
B
C
D
E
F
G
H
I
J
K
L
M
N
O
P
Q
R
S
T
U
V
W
X
Y
Z

My 2 in 1 Animal Picture Dictionary A to Z pages

make believe ideas

a
b
c
d
e
f
g
h
i
j
k
l
m
n
o
p
q
r
s
t
u
v
w
x
y
z

Aa

amphibian

Amphibians begin life under water, but change as they grow, so they can breathe air and live on land, too.

animal

An **animal** is somethin that lives and moves around. Eagles, goldfis spiders, and rabbits are all animals.

albatross

Albatrosses are big seabirds that spend most of their life in the air.

ant

Ants are tiny insects that live together in big groups called colonies.

alligator

Alligators live in swamps and have long tails, short legs, and fierce snapping jaws.

angelfish

Colorful **angelfish** often live in warm seas. Their flat body makes it hard for enemies to see them from the front.

antelope

Antelopes are deer-like animals with long horns on their head.

antennae

Lots of insects have two **antennae** on their head to help them to smell and taste.

B b

antler

The horns on a male deer's head are called **antlers**.

baboon

Baboons are monkeys that live in big groups. They sleep sitting up to watch for danger.

bat

A **bat** is a small, furry nighttime animal that looks like a mouse with wings. Bats hang upside down when they sleep.

ape

An **ape** looks like a monkey, but has no tail.

badger

Badgers are night-time animals that eat small animals, fruit, and worms.

beak

A **beak** is the hard part of a bird's mouth.

bear

A **bear** is a big, heavy animal with thick fur and sharp claws. Bears sleep for most of the winter.

bee

A **bee** is an insect with wings. Bees make honey.

beetle

A **beetle** is an insect with hard, shiny wing covers. Ladybugs are beetles.

bird

Birds have wings, feathers, and a beak. Most birds can fly.

bison

Giant American **bison** live in herds on the grasslands of North America. Their shaggy coat keeps out the winter cold.

beaver

Beavers live in lakes and rivers and are good swimmers. They build dams in streams to make their homes.

bill

A bird uses its **bill** to eat, build a nest, and smooth its feathers.

boa constrictor

Boa constrictors are long snakes that wind themselves around their prey to squeeze it to death.

buffalo

Buffalo are large, cow-like animals that live in groups called herds. They have big horns.

Cc

bull

A **bull** is a big, male animal of the cow family. Most bulls have horns.

calf

A **calf** is a young cow or bull. Calves drink milk for the first few months.

budgerigar

Budgerigars are small birds that live in big flocks in the wild. People often keep budgies as pets.

butterfly

A **butterfly** is an insect with four large wings.

camel

A **camel** is an animal with one or two humps on its back.

camouflage

Camouflage is when an animal hides from danger by blending in with the things around it.

cat

A **cat** is an animal with soft fur, sharp claws, and a long tail. People keep small cats as pets. Lions and tigers are called big cats.

cattle

Cows, buffalo, and oxen are all kinds of **cattle**. Male cattle are bulls, females are cows, and babies are calves.

caribou

Caribou is the North American name for reindeer. Caribou have antlers and live near the icy North Pole.

centipede

A **centipede** is a creature with lots of tiny legs.

caterpillar

A **caterpillar** looks like a worm with legs. It turns into a butterfly or moth.

chameleon

A **chameleon** is a lizard that lives in trees. Chameleons can change color.

cheetah

Cheetahs are big wild cats, with spotted coats. They are the fastest runners in the world.

chicken

A **chicken** is a bird that farmers keep for eggs and meat. A male chicken is a cockerel and a female is a hen.

claw

A **claw** is the sharp, curved nail on the foot of a bird or animal.

chimpanzee

Chimpanzees are apes that live in big family groups. They eat and sleep in the trees.

cobra

A **cobra** is a kind of snake with poisonous fangs. One bite can kill.

chick

A **chick** is a baby bird.

chipmunk

Chipmunks are small, striped squirrels. They have a bushy tail and eat nuts.

a b c d e f g h i j k l m n o p q r s t u v w x y z

A B C D E F G H I J K L M N O P Q R S T U V W X Y Z

cockerel

A **cockerel** is a male chicken.

cow

A **cow** is a large farm animal. People drink its milk.

crocodile

A **crocodile** is a reptile with sharp teeth, short legs, and a long tail.

cockle

A **cockle** is a kind of shellfish that has two fanlike shells joined together.

coyote

Also called prairie wolves, **coyotes** live on the dry, grassy American plains.

crow

A **crow** is a big, black bird.

coral

Corals are tiny sea creatures. When some corals die, they leave a hard skeleton.

crab

Most **crabs** live in or near water and have a hard shell, eyes on stalks, and big claws.

cub

Young lions, tigers, foxes, and bears are called **cubs**.

Dd

dingo
A **dingo** is a wild dog from Australia.

dolphin
Dolphins are sea mammals. They have to hold their breath under water.

dog
A **dog** is an animal that barks. Dogs are often kept as pets. Foxes, jackals, and wolves are wild dogs.

donkey
A **donkey** is a kind of small horse with long ears. Donkeys are used to carry people and things over rough paths.

deer
Deer are shy animals that can run very fast. Male deer, called stags, have branched horns, or antlers. Female deer are called does, and the babies are fawns.

a b c d e f g h i j k l m n o p q r s t u v w x y z

Left margin: A B C D E F G H I J K L M N O P Q R S T U V W X Y Z

dragonfly

A **dragonfly** is a big flying insect that lives near water.

Ee

eel

An **eel** is a long, slimy, snakelike fish.

duck

A **duck** is a bird that lives near water. Ducks have waterproof feathers and webbed feet for swimming.

eagle

An **eagle** is a large bird with big wings, a curved beak, and sharp claws for killing its prey.

egg

Birds, fish, snakes, and lizards live inside **eggs** until they are big enough to hatch out.

duckling

A **duckling** is a young duck.

ears

Most animals have two **ears** on the top or side of their head for hearing sounds.

elephant

An **elephant** is a large, gray animal with big ears and a long trunk.

elephant seal

Elephant seals live in the freezing ocean near the South Pole.

elk

Also called red deer, **elk** live in American forests and have huge antlers.

eye

Animals have eyes to see with. Most animals have two **eyes**, but some, like spiders, have as many as eight!

Ff

feather

Birds have **feathers** on their body to keep them warm and dry. Wing feathers also help birds fly.

fish

A **fish** is a scaly animal that lives in water. Fish have gills for breathing under water.

flamingo

A **flamingo** is a tall, pink bird with very long legs for wading in water at the edge of lakes.

flock

A **flock** is a group of birds or sheep.

a b c d e f g h i j k l m n o p q r s t u v w x y z

fly

A **fly** is a small insect with one pair of wings. There are lots of different kinds of fly.

fox

A **fox** is a kind of wild dog with a long, bushy tail. Foxes hunt mainly at night.

Gg

foal

A **foal** is a young horse. Foals can stand up as soon as they are born. Young zebras and donkeys are also called foals.

frog

A **frog** is a small amphibian that lives in ponds and damp places. Some frogs live high in the treetops.

fur

Fur is the thick, soft hair that covers some animals.

gazelle

Gazelles are long-legged antelopes that can run fast. They live in big herds on the grasslands of Africa. They have long, unbranched horns on their head.

gerbil

A **gerbil** is a small animal with long, back legs and very soft fur. Children often keep gerbils as pets.

gibbon

Gibbons are small apes. They use their long arms to swing through the trees.

gills

Gills are the flaps of skin behind a fish's eye that let it breathe under water.

giraffe

A **giraffe** is a tall animal with long legs and a very long neck.

goat

Goats have long hair and horns.

goldfish

A **goldfish** is a small, golden-orange fish. People often keep pet goldfish.

goose

A **goose** is a large bird with a long neck that lives near water. A male goose is a gander, and a baby goose is a gosling.

a b c d e f g h i j k l m n o p q r s t u v w x y z

A B C D E F G H I J K L M N O P Q R S T U V W X Y Z

gorilla

A **gorilla** is a strong, heavy ape with long arms for swinging in trees. Gorillas live in big family groups in African forests.

grasshopper

Grasshoppers are insects with strong back legs for jumping. They rub their back legs together to make a big noise.

Hh

guinea pig

A **guinea pig** is a small, furry animal with short legs and no tail.

hamster

A **hamster** is a small, furry animal with pockets inside its cheeks where it stores food.

gosling

A **gosling** is a young goose.

gull

Gulls are big birds that usually live near the sea. They catch fish with their long beak.

hare

A **hare** is like a big rabbit, with strong bac legs and long ears.

hawk

A **hawk** is a bird of prey with sharp claws and a curved, pointed beak for catching and eating meat.

hen

A **hen** is a female chicken. Hens lay eggs.

heron

Herons are large birds that live near rivers and lakes. They have long legs for wading, and long, sharp beaks for catching fish.

herd

A **herd** is a big group of animals, such as zebras, buffalo, cows, and deer.

hippopotamus

Hippopotamuses are big animals that love to wallow in muddy African rivers.

hedgehog

Hedgehogs are small, spiny nighttime animals. When they are scared, they roll into a ball.

hoof

A **hoof** is the hard part of a horse's foot. Pigs and deer have hooves, too.

horn

Sheep, cattle, and antelope have hollow **horns** for fighting other animals.

horse

A **horse** is a big animal with hooves. People ride horses and use them to pull heavy loads. Zebras and donkeys are kinds of horses.

hummingbird

Hummingbirds are tiny birds that sip sweet flower nectar through their long, pointed beak. They can hover in the air and even fly backward.

hornbill

A **hornbill** is a bird with a big bill that has a kind of horn on top.

human

A **human** is a man, woman, or child.

hyena

Hyenas are doglike meat eaters that usually hunt at night.

Ii

iguana

An **iguana** is a large lizard that lives in trees in hot countries.

insects

An **insect** is a small animal with six legs. Many insects have wings. Butterflies, flies, and beetles are all insects.

Jj

jaguar

A **jaguar's** spotted coat helps it hide from its prey in the forest.

jellyfish

Jellyfish are soft sea creatures with no bones, and stinging tentacles.

Kk

kangaroo

Kangaroos are big Australian animals with strong back legs for jumping.

kid

A **kid** is a young goat. Children are often called kids, too.

kitten

A **kitten** is a young cat.

Ll

leg

Animals need **legs** to get around. Some animals, like you, have only two legs, while others, like millipedes, have lots.

Koala

Koalas are night-time animals from Australia that live, sleep, and feed in eucalyptus trees.

ladybug

A **ladybug** is a small flying beetle. Most ladybugs are red with black spots.

lemur

Lemurs live in big groups in forest on the island of Madagascar.

lamb

A **lamb** is a young sheep that is still with its mother.

leopard

A **leopard** is a big wild cat with spots on its coat.

limpet

A **limpet** is a shellfish that looks like a tiny Chinese hat. Limpets stick to rocks under the sea.

llama

Llamas are camel-like animals with long fur.

Mm

lion

Lions are big wild cats that live on the African plains.

lobster

Lobsters live on the seafloor, where they hunt for food at night. They have eight legs and two sharp claws.

macaw

A **macaw** is a kind of parrot. Macaws have a strong, hooked beak for cracking open seeds and nuts.

lizard

A **lizard** is a reptile with a long body, four legs, scaly skin, and a long tail.

lynx

A **lynx** is a wild cat with long legs, a short tail, and tufted ears.

mammal

A **mammal** is an animal that feeds its babies with its own milk. Mammals do not lay eggs and often have hair or fur on their body. Cats, goats, dolphins, and people are all mammals.

mane

A **mane** is the long hair that grows on the back of the neck and head of animals like lions and horses.

mare

A **mare** is a female horse. Female zebras and donkeys are also called mares.

marsupial

Marsupials are mammals like koalas and kangaroos whose babies are born very young. The baby crawls to a pouch on its mother's tummy where it grows.

millipede

A **millipede** is a creature with lots of tiny legs. Millipede means "a thousand feet."

mole

Small, velvety **moles** have shovel-like front feet for digging tunnels in the ground.

mongoose

A **mongoose** is a small, fast, meat-eating animal that catches insects and lizards.

monkey

Monkeys have strong arms and long tails to swing from tree to tree.

moth

A **moth** is a night-time insect with four big wings. You often see moths fluttering around lights.

moose

A **moose** is the biggest kind of deer. Male moose have huge antlers, which they lose every autumn.

mouse

A **mouse** is a small, furry animal with a long tail. Mice have sharp front teeth for gnawing food.

mussel

A **mussel** is a kind of shellfish that has two long oval shells that are joined together.

Nn

nest

A **nest** is the home that animals like birds and mice make for their babies.

newt

Newts are lizardlike amphibians, which means they can breathe when they are in water and when they are out of it.

Oo

octopus

An **octopus** is a sea animal with a soft body and eight long arms.

orangutan

Orangutans are big apes with reddish fur and long arms.

ostrich

Ostriches are the world's biggest birds and are bigger than a human. They cannot fly but are very fast runners.

otter

Otters live near water and are very good swimmers with strong, webbed back feet.

owl

An **owl** is a bird that hunts for small animals at night. It has big eyes to help it see in the dark.

oyster

An **oyster** is a shellfish that has two shells joined together. Pearls grow inside oyster shells.

P p

parrot

A **parrot** is a bird with brightly colored feathers and a sharp, curved beak for eating seeds. Some parrots can talk.

pack

A **pack** is a group of dogs or wolves that live and hunt together.

peacock

A **peacock** is a bird. Male peacocks can open out their beautiful tail feathers into a shimmering fan.

panda

Pandas look like big, black-and-white bears. Their favorite food is bamboo shoots.

paw

A **paw** is an animal's foot.

pelican

A **pelican** is a large, fish-eating bird with a big, pouched bill.

penguin

A **penguin** is a black-and-white seabird that lives in big colonies on cold, rocky coastlines. Penguins can't fly. Instead, they use their flipper-like wings for swimming after fish in the sea.

pheasant

Pheasants are big, often brightly colored birds that like to run instead of fly.

pig

A **pig** is an animal with a fat body, short legs, and a short curly tail.

pigeon

A **pigeon** is a bird that makes a soft, cooing sound. Pigeons live in woods, towns and cities.

piglet

A **piglet** is a young pig.

polar bear

A **polar bear** is a big, white bear that lives on the ice and snow near the North Pole.

pony
A **pony** is a small horse.

prey
Prey is any animal that is hunted and eaten by another animal.

puppy
A **puppy** is a young dog. Puppies love to chew things and can get into trouble!

porcupine
A **porcupine** has long spines. If it is attacked, it sticks its spines into its enemy.

puffin
A **puffin** is a seabird with a short, curved beak. Puffins build nests in cliffs.

predator
A **predator** hunts and kills other animals for food.

puma
A **puma** is a big wild cat. It is also called a cougar, panther, or mountain lion.

python
A **python** is a kind of snake that squeezes its prey to death.

a b c d e f g h i j k l m n o p q r s t u v w x y z

Rr

rat

Rats look like mice, but bigger. They eat almost anything.

reindeer

Reindeer have antlers and live in the icy north.

rabbit

Small, furry **rabbits** have long ears and a fluffy white tail.

rattlesnake

A **rattlesnake** has a rattle on its tail, which it shakes when it is angry.

reptile

Reptiles have scaly skin and short legs, or no legs at all. Crocodiles, lizards, tortoises, and snakes are all kinds of reptile. Reptiles lay eggs.

raccoon

A **raccoon** has a striped tail and face markings that look like a mask.

ray

A **ray** is a flat fish with a long tail. Rays flap their fins like wings under water.

rhinoceros

A **rhinoceros** is a big animal with tough, leathery skin and horns on its head.

Ss

scorpion

A **scorpion** has eight legs and a deadly sting at the end of its tail.

salmon

A **salmon** is a kind of fish that lives in the sea but swims up rivers to lay its eggs.

sea anemone

A **sea anemone** is a sea creature that has stinging tentacles to catch its prey.

rodent

Rodents have two strong front teeth for gnawing. Mice, rats, gerbils, and hamsters are all rodents.

scale

Scales are small, thin, flexible plates that protect the skin of animals like fish and reptiles.

seahorse

Seahorses are fish with a long snout and curled tail for holding on to weeds. They swim slowly with their head upright.

abcdefghijklmnopqrstuvwxyz

seal

Seals are sea animals with flippers for swimming. They hold their breath to swim under water.

shark

A **shark** is a big fish. Some sharks have very sharp teeth and are fierce underwater hunters.

shell

A **shell** is a hard covering around something. Shellfish have shells around them to protect their soft bodies.

sea lion

Sea lions live by the sea. They swim well but can also walk on land.

sheep

A **sheep** is an animal with a thick, woolly coat. Farmers raise sheep for their meat, wool, and milk.

sea urchin

Sea urchins cling to rocks on the seabed, eating tiny seaweeds or animals. Sharp spines keep enemies away.

shellfish

A **shellfish** is a soft-bodied animal that lives inside a shell. Some shellfish, like scallops, live between two shells.

skin

The **outer** covering of an animal's body is its skin. Skin may be covered in fur, feathers, or scales.

slug

A **slug** has no bones and is like a snail with no shell. As slugs creep along, they leave a slimy trail.

spider

A **spider** is a creature with eight legs. Most spiders spin webs to catch insects for food.

skunk

When a **skunk** is attacked, it squirts a bad-smelling liquid at its enemy.

snail

A **snail** is a small, soft animal that lives inside a spiral shell. Snails move slowly and leave a slimy trail.

sponge

Sponges are sea animals that feed on tiny animals and plants in the water.

sloth

Sloths are slow animals that spend their lives hanging upside down in trees.

snake

A **snake** is a scaly reptile with a long body and no legs. Some snakes have a deadly bite.

squirrel

Small, furry **squirrels** live in trees. They have bushy tails and eat nuts.

a b c d e f g h i j k l m n o p q r s t u v w x y z

stag

A **stag** is a male deer. Stags have antlers.

stick insect

Stick insects are camouflaged to look just like the sticks and leaves where they live. They can even change color.

Tt

stallion

A **stallion** is a male horse.

swan

A **swan** is a large bird with a long, curved neck. Swans live on rivers and lakes.

tail

An animal's **tail** is the part that grows out from the end of its back.

starfish

A **starfish** is a star-shaped animal with five arms that lives in the ocean.

tapir

Tapirs live in forests. They have a short trunk for tearing leaves off branches.

terrapin

A **terrapin** is a small reptile with short legs and a shell on its back. Terrapins live in lakes, rivers, and swamps.

toad

A **toad** is a small, frog-like amphibian that lives in ponds and damp places.

tree frog

Tree frogs live in trees. Suckers on their feet help them stick to the branches.

tiger

A **tiger** is a big, wild cat with orange fur and black stripes. Wild tigers are rare, but some still live in India and China.

tortoise

A **tortoise** is a slow-moving reptile with short legs and a big shell on its back.

turkey

Turkeys are large birds that nest on the ground. Farmers keep turkeys for their meat.

toucan

A **toucan** is a bird with black and white feathers. and a large bill.

turtle

A **turtle** is a reptile that lives in water. Turtles have short legs and a shell on their back.

a b c d e f g h i j k l m n o p q r s t u v w x y z

U u

V v

W w

whale

A **whale** is a large sea animal. Unlike a fish, it breathes air through a blowhole on the top of its head.

udder

An **udder** is the part of a cow where the milk comes out to feed her calf.

walrus

A **walrus** is a fat, wrinkly sea animal. Walruses have whiskers and tusks.

wildebeest

Wildebeest are big antelopes that live in herds on the African plains. They are also called gnus.

vulture

A **vulture** is a big bird that eats dead animals.

wasp

A **wasp** is a flying insect with black and yellow stripes. Wasps have a sting.

wing

A **wing** is the part of an insect or bird that it uses for flying.

wolf

A **wolf** is a kind of wild dog. Wolves live together in a big group called a pack.

Yy Zz

woodpecker

Woodpeckers have a sharp beak to peck out insects from bark.

zebra

A **zebra** looks like a horse with black and white stripes. Zebras live in Africa.

worm

A **worm** is a small, soft animal with a long body and no legs. Earthworms live in the ground.

yak

A **yak** is a large, cowlike animal with lots of shaggy hair and long horns.

a b c d e f g h i j k l m n o p q r s t u v w x y z

Parks and gardens

All kinds of animals live in parks and gardens in our towns and cities. Some hide themselves, while others show off all day long.

wasp

slug

Question

How many insects can you see here?

bee

rat

peacock

pigeon

squirrel

mole

shovel-like hands

ladybug

Did you Know?

When a skunk is frightened, it does a handstand, sticks its bottom in the air and makes a horrible smell!

fluffy tail

white stripe

snail

skunk

Answer
Three! The ladybug, bee, and wasp.

Fields and woodland

Woodland trees and shrubs make a great hiding place for animals. They also provide plenty of fruits, nuts, and seeds to eat.

crow

Question

How many babies can a mouse have in a year?

badger

fox

warm fur

millipede

bushy tail

butterflies

beetle

spider

deer

leg

Did you know?

Spiders have eight legs and up to eight eyes! They spin fantastic webs to catch flies, which they poison and suck to death!

woodpecker

moth

chipmunk

hedgehog

mouse

worm

Answer
Over a hundred! That's 10 litters of 10 to 12 babies!

11

Deep in the forest

All kinds of animals live in the deep, dark forest. They eat fruits, nuts, and leaves as well as insects and other, smaller animals.

lynx

hummingbird

belly

fur

Question

Why do bears sleep in winter?

ant

raccoon

paw   bear   sharp claw

elk

wolf

eagle

Did you know?

If a porcupine is attacked, it rattles its spine, then charges backward and stabs its spines into its enemy's face! Ouch!

porcupine

moose

Answer
Because snow covers the ground and there is no food.

13

Ponds and rivers

Rivers and ponds teem with animal life. Fish swim in the water, while other animals live on the bank – waiting to catch their lunch.

salmon

duck

Question

How far can a frog jump?

dragonfly

otters

frog

beaver

Did you know?

Beavers dam streams with piles of branches, mud, and stones to make a pond. The pond keeps enemies away from their stick house, called a lodge.

heron

Answer
A frog can jump up to 20 times its own length!

tail

eye

back

newt

Lakes and swamps

Birds swim on lakes, fish swim in them, and lots of animals enjoy life on the edge. Swamps are great for crocodiles and hippos to hide!

turtle

pelican

crocodile

strong tail

sharp teeth

scaly skin

Question

Why are a hippo's eyes, ears and nose on top of its head?

goose

Did you know?
Flamingos are only pink because of the red coloring in the food they eat!

flamingo

swan

trout

toad

Answer
So it can see, hear, smell, and breathe under water.

hippopotamus

belly

Cliffs and seashores

The beach and high, rocky cliffs that rise up above are home to lots of animals. Some, like seals, like living a long way from people.

mussel

Question

How many legs does a crab have?

seagull

sea lions

whiskers

ear

crab

sea anemone

cockleshell

sea urchins

claws.
form big pincer-like
Ten! The front pair
Answer

puffin

starfish

Did you know?

Starfish don't have a head or a brain. Their five arms are strong enough to force open a shellfish and suck out its body.

flipper

waterproof fur

seal

In the ocean

The deep waters of the ocean are full of fish of all colors and sizes. But there are lots of other interesting animals, like lobsters, turtles, and dolphins.

angelfish

seahorse

eel

lobster

jellyfish

dolphin

Question

Is a dolphin a fish?

shark

turtle

Did you know?

Sharks are underwater meat-eaters and have strong jaws with lots of very sharp, sawlike teeth. One bite from a shark is usually enough to kill.

wing

tail

whale

ray

Answer
No, it isn't, it's a mammal and it needs to breathe air.

octopus

coral

Wide open spaces

Lots of animals live on big, grassy plains. Some, like zebra and giraffes, eat grass and leaves. Others, like lions, hunt and kill other animals.

vulture

bison

leopard

wildebeest

grasshopper

Question

Why does a giraffe have a long neck?

lion

baboon

Did you know?

Elephants are the biggest and heaviest animals on land. An adult elephant weighs more than 200 children.

elephant

zebra

antelope

Answer
So it can eat leaves from high up in the trees.

rhinoceros

giraffe

In the rainforest

The hot, steamy rainforest is home to lots of animals. Some live high in the treetops, while others look for food on the ground.

stick insect

Question

How does a stick insect hide in the forest?

tapir

tree frog

orangutan

hornbill

Did you know?

Orangutan means "man of the woods" in the Malay language. Can you guess why?

parrot

tree snake

chimpanzee

tiger

Answer
By looking and
behaving exactly
like a stick!

chameleon

gorilla

toucan

large,
colorful
bill

Hot and dry

Some animals are able to live in very hot and dry places. Many sleep or rest in the shade during the day and come out at night when it is cooler.

Question

What does a rattlesnake use its tail rattle for?

rattlesnake

lizard

ostrich

feathers

beak

scorpion

strong legs

camel

kangaroo

coyote

mongoose

koala

Did you know?

The cheetah is the world's fastest land mammal. It can run as fast as a bus!

spotted coat

cheetah

Answer
To warn enemies that it is ready to attack – one bite can kill!

27

Mountains, snow, and ice

Thick, shaggy fur and plenty of fat help lots of animals keep warm in the snow and ice of some of the world's coldest places.

seal

puma

reindeer

penguin

Did you know?

Penguins are birds, but they cannot fly. Instead, they use their wings as flippers for swimming fast through the water.

panda

Question

Why are polar bears white?

walrus

llama

yak

albatross

Answer
So their enemies
cannot easily see
them in the snow.

polar bears

Animal babies

Baby animals often have different names from their parents. Kids can be baby goats or children, and cubs can be baby bears, lions, tigers, or wolves.

Question

Where do chicks come from?

piglet

puppy

kitten

gosling

duckling

Answer

Chicks hatch out of eggs!

kid

chick

cub

woolly coat

lamb

foal

Did you know?

A newborn foal can stand up as soon as it is born. The first thing it does is have a drink of its mother's milk.